TEXAS RANGERS

ALL-TIME GREATS

BY ETHAN OLSON

Book design by Jake Slavik
Cover design by Jake Slavik

Photographs ©: Peter Joneleit/Icon Sportswire/AP Images, cover (top), 1 (top); Tom DiPace/AP Images, cover (bottom), 1 (bottom); Focus on Sport/Getty Images Sport/Getty Images, 4, 7; Mitchell Layton/Getty Images Sport/Getty Images, 9, 16; Ron Vesely/MLB Photos/Getty Images Sport/Getty Images, 10, 15; Ronald Martinez/Getty Images Sport/Getty Images, 12, 19; Jonathan Daniel/Getty Images Sport/Getty Images, 21

Press Box Books, an imprint of Press Room Editions.

ISBN
978-1-63494-801-2 (library bound)
978-1-63494-821-0 (paperback)
978-1-63494-859-3 (epub)
978-1-63494-841-8 (hosted ebook)

Library of Congress Control Number: 2023910391

Distributed by North Star Editions, Inc.
2297 Waters Drive
Mendota Heights, MN 55120
www.northstareditions.com

Printed in the United States of America
012024

ABOUT THE AUTHOR

Ethan Olson is a sportswriter and editor based in Minneapolis.

TABLE OF CONTENTS

HOWARD
33

CHAPTER 1
A TRIP DOWN SOUTH

The Texas Rangers played their first Major League Baseball (MLB) season in 1961. But the team played in a different location with a different name. It started out in Washington, DC, as the Senators. While the team struggled to win games, it did have stars.

Mammoth outfielder **Frank Howard** was one of them. Standing 6-foot-7 (201 cm), the "Washington Monument" was an intimidating presence at the plate. His size helped him crush balls. A few of his home runs landed in the upper deck of Washington's RFK Stadium. Howard used his power to lead the Senators in homers and runs batted in (RBIs) each of his seven seasons with the team.

Joining Howard in the outfield was **Jeff Burroughs**. The Senators selected the talented prospect first overall in the 1969 MLB Draft. Burroughs debuted with the Senators in 1970 and moved with the team when it became the Texas Rangers in 1972. Burroughs had his best season in 1974. He led the American League (AL) in RBIs and won the AL Most Valuable Player (MVP) Award.

MAGICAL MANAGER

Ted Williams had a Hall of Fame career as an outfielder with the Boston Red Sox. Then in 1969, he worked magic in his first season as Washington's manager. The Senators won 86 games. That was 21 more than they'd won the previous year. Thanks to Williams's coaching, the team dramatically improved in almost every offensive category.

JENKINS
31

Even after the move, the Rangers didn't have much success. They traded for pitcher **Fergie Jenkins** before the 1974 season. The righty helped Texas improve. He won a team-record 25 games that season.

Jim Sundberg also made his Rangers debut in 1974. The catcher paired perfectly with Jenkins and became one of the league's best defenders at his position. Sundberg's skill behind the plate and strong arm helped him earn six straight Gold Gloves with Texas. That award is given to the best defensive player at each position.

Righty **Charlie Hough** improved the team when he joined in 1980. His knuckleballs stunned opposing hitters. Before he left in 1990, Hough's name was all over the Rangers record books.

CAREER STRIKEOUTS
RANGERS TEAM RECORD
Charlie Hough: 1,452

RYAN
34

While Hough was known for his knucklers, **Nolan Ryan** struck fear in batters with his fastball. After joining Texas in 1989, he pitched two no-hitters with the Rangers. And on August 22, 1989, Ryan recorded his 5,000th career strikeout. He was the first player in MLB history to reach that mark.

SIERRA
21

CHAPTER 2
DIVISION-WINNING DREAMS

Right fielder **Rubén Sierra** helped lead a new era in Texas. Sierra impressed right away as a rookie in 1986. In just his second career at bat, Sierra smashed a home run. Three years later, Sierra had his best season. He led the AL with 119 RBIs, 14 triples, and 4 total bases.

The Rangers drafted **Kenny Rogers** as an outfielder. But his powerful left arm gave him promise as a pitcher. After four seasons as a reliever, Rogers became a starting pitcher in 1993. A year later, he made headlines by throwing the 14th perfect game in MLB history.

Fan favorite **Rusty Greer** provided strong defense for the Rangers. The outfielder would

sacrifice his body to make incredible catches. None were more significant than in 1994, when he made a diving grab to keep Rogers's perfect game alive.

Texas traded for **Rafael Palmeiro** before the 1989 season. The first baseman could hit for both power and contact. In his 10 seasons with Texas, he had years in which he led the AL in hits, runs, and doubles. He finished his career ranked second on the Rangers' all-time home runs list.

Only **Juan González** hit more home runs for the Rangers. The outfielder led the AL in home runs in 1992 and 1993. González then hit 47 homers in 1996 on his way to winning the AL MVP Award. He also propelled the Rangers into the playoffs for the first time in the team's history. Two years later, González earned his second AL MVP while leading the league with 157 RBIs.

STAT SPOTLIGHT

CAREER HOME RUNS
RANGERS TEAM RECORD

Juan González: 372

Iván Rodríguez followed up González's MVP season with one of his own. In 1999, the catcher slugged 35 home runs and racked up 113 RBIs. Behind González and Rodríguez, the Rangers went back to the playoffs in 1998 and 1999.

While Rodríguez was a great hitter, his biggest strength was his defense. "Pudge" could throw runners out with ease from home plate. That helped him earn 10 straight Gold Gloves with the Rangers.

TEXAS HEAT

Texas summers are scorching hot. And for many years, the Rangers played in an outdoor ballpark. One writer described the outfield stands at Arlington Stadium as the "world's largest open-air roaster." In 2020, the Rangers moved to a new, retractable-roof stadium. Now fans can sit in air-conditioned comfort when the weather is too extreme.

RODRIGUEZ
3

CHAPTER 3
REACHING NEW HEIGHTS

Before the 2001 season, the Rangers signed **Alex Rodriguez** to the largest contract in American professional sports history. The star shortstop made the most of his three years with Texas. Rodriguez led the AL in home runs in all three seasons. He also led the league in runs twice.

When Rodriguez left, **Michael Young** took over as the starting shortstop for Texas. Young was an elite hitter in his own right. In 2005, he won the AL batting title with an average of .331.

Second baseman **Ian Kinsler** had both power and speed. In 2009, Kinsler racked up 30 home runs and 30 stolen bases in the same season. And in 2011, he did it again. Kinsler was just the 12th player in MLB history to do so more than once.

Rounding out a stacked lineup was **Josh Hamilton**. The outfielder put fear in the minds of opposing pitchers. During one game in 2008, the Tampa Bay Rays intentionally walked Hamilton with the bases loaded. That hadn't happened in the AL in 107 years. In 2010, Hamilton was even better. He won the AL MVP

CAREER HITS
RANGERS TEAM RECORD
Michael Young: 2,230

Award after leading the league with a .359 batting average.

Young moved to third base after **Elvis Andrus** debuted in 2009. The energetic shortstop was a major threat on the basepaths. Andrus stole 30 or more bases in five different seasons with Texas. The Rangers made it to the 2010 World Series with this group of players. They ended up losing the series in five games. However, Texas made it back to the World Series in 2011.

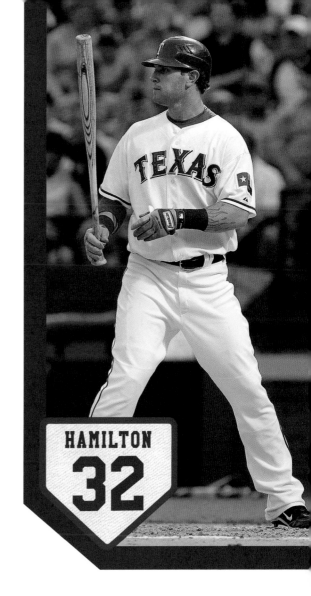

Power hitter **Adrián Beltré** was one reason why. The third baseman earned his first of three Gold Gloves with Texas in 2011. Then he came up clutch in the World Series. In Game 6, Beltré smacked a tiebreaking home run in the seventh inning. However, it wasn't enough. Texas lost the series in seven games.

The Rangers added another star before the 2012 season when they signed **Yu Darvish** from Japan. The starter's fastballs were difficult for hitters to

SPENDING SPREE

Before the 2022 season, the Rangers upgraded their infield in free agency. They signed shortstop Corey Seager and second baseman Marcus Semien. Both were former All-Stars. Before the 2023 season, Texas signed superstar pitcher Jacob deGrom. Rangers fans hoped these stars would keep the team competitive for years to come.

DARVISH
11

deal with. And in 2013, Darvish led the AL with
277 strikeouts. Texas fans knew they got to see
special talent whenever Darvish pitched.

TIMELINE

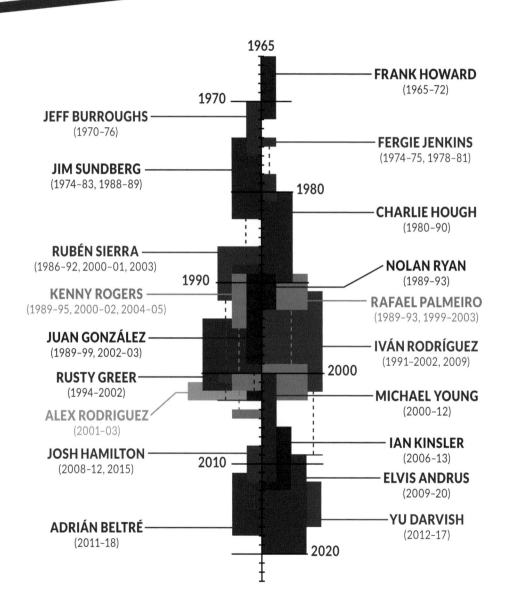

1965

FRANK HOWARD
(1965–72)

1970

JEFF BURROUGHS
(1970–76)

FERGIE JENKINS
(1974–75, 1978–81)

JIM SUNDBERG
(1974–83, 1988–89)

1980

CHARLIE HOUGH
(1980–90)

RUBÉN SIERRA
(1986–92, 2000–01, 2003)

NOLAN RYAN
(1989–93)

1990

KENNY ROGERS
(1989–95, 2000–02, 2004–05)

RAFAEL PALMEIRO
(1989–93, 1999–2003)

JUAN GONZÁLEZ
(1989–99, 2002–03)

IVÁN RODRÍGUEZ
(1991–2002, 2009)

RUSTY GREER
(1994–2002)

2000

ALEX RODRIGUEZ
(2001–03)

MICHAEL YOUNG
(2000–12)

IAN KINSLER
(2006–13)

JOSH HAMILTON
(2008–12, 2015)

2010

ELVIS ANDRUS
(2009–20)

ADRIÁN BELTRÉ
(2011–18)

YU DARVISH
(2012–17)

2020

TEXAS RANGERS

Team history: Washington Senators (1961–71), Texas Rangers (1972–)

World Series titles: 0*

Key managers:

Johnny Oates (1995–2001)
506–476 (.515)

Bobby Valentine (1985–92)
581–605 (.490)

Ron Washington (2007–14)
664–611 (.521)

MORE INFORMATION

To learn more about the Texas Rangers, go to **pressboxbooks.com/AllAccess**.

These links are routinely monitored and updated to provide the most current information available.

*through 2022

GLOSSARY

clutch
Able to perform well in important or pressure-packed situations.

contract
A written agreement that keeps a player with a team for a certain amount of time.

debut
To make a first appearance.

elite
The best of the best.

free agency
A period in the off-season when teams can sign players who do not have a contract with a team.

no-hitter
A game in which a pitcher, or combination of pitchers, doesn't allow any hits.

perfect game
A game in which a pitcher doesn't allow any batters to reach base.

rookie
A first-year player.

INDEX

From the legends of the game to today's superstars, Major League Baseball has always been home to supremely talented players. Get to know the greatest players from baseball's best teams.

BOOKS IN THIS SERIES

ARIZONA **DIAMONDBACKS**

BALTIMORE **ORIOLES**

CLEVELAND **GUARDIANS**

COLORADO **ROCKIES**

DETROIT **TIGERS**

KANSAS CITY **ROYALS**

LOS ANGELES **ANGELS**

MIAMI **MARLINS**

PITTSBURGH **PIRATES**

TEXAS **RANGERS**

SPECIAL FEATURES:

- Informative sidebars
- Team facts
- Timeline
- Glossary
- Additional resources
- Index

PRESS BOX BOOKS

ISBN: 978-1-63494-821-0

90000

9 781634 948210